Bra
phrasebook

Mark Balla

Brazilian Phrasebook
2nd edition

Published by
Lonely Planet Publications
Head Office: PO Box 617, Hawthorn, Vic 3122, Australia
Branches: 155 Filbert St, Suite 251, Oakland, CA 94607, USA
10 Barley Mow Passage, Chiswick, London W4 4PH, UK
71 bis rue du Cardinal Lemoine, 75005 Paris, France
Printed by
Colorcraft Ltd, Hong Kong

About This Book
Mark Balla wrote the Brazilian phrasebook, 1st edition. This edition has been
completely revised by Gracila Stone. Sally Steward edited the book and
Margaret Jung was responsible for the design and cover.

Published
February 1993

National Library of Australia Cataloguing in Publication Data

Balla, Mark
Brazilian Phrasebook.

Rev. ed.
ISBN 0 86442 176 1

1. Portuguese language - Brazil - Conversation and phrase books -
English. I. Title.

469.798

Contents

Introduction

Brazil has a population of some 150 million, almost all of whom speak Portuguese (or *brasileiro* as it is known by many). Those who don't speak the national language are either recent immigrants or members of certain isolated native American tribes in the Amazon region. Around the borders of Uruguay and Argentina are Spanish-speaking communities, and near the Paraguayan border there are speakers of Guarani, one of Paraguay's two national languages.

There has been a number of developments in the Brazilian language since the Portuguese arrived around the beginning of the 16th century. The main changes are related to vocabulary and pronunciation, and came about due to various African and native American influences – influences that were also important in the development of Brazilian culture. African influences, brought about by the slave trade with Portugal's colonies of São Tomé, Guinea-Bissau, Angola and other coastal regions of Africa, can be felt today in, among other things, the music of Brazil. Other influences are present in the large Japanese and Korean communities of the São Paulo and Rio states and, further south, in European communities from countries such as Germany and Italy.

Brazilians are famous for their parties, and no discussion of Brazil would be complete without a mention of Carnival, *Carnaval*. Taking place in February or March, Carnival is not limited to Rio de Janeiro. In fact, you would be hard pressed to find a city or town which does not get caught up in this madcap week of lunacy. Processions, dancing, all-night partying, drinking and general debauchery almost bring the country to a standstill for nearly a week of festivities. In reality, the partying begins long before and ends weeks after the official Carnival period.

Finally, it has become very fashionable for wealthy Brazilians to take courses in English at one of the numerous private language schools that have sprung up throughout the country. However, with so little opportunity to practice, there are not many people outside the major cities who can get by in English. Certainly the visitor who has any Portuguese is a step ahead of the rest.

Abbreviations Used in This Book

f	feminine
inf	informal
lit	literally
m	masculine
pl	plural
sg	singular

Pronunciation

Portuguese pronunciation can be rather tricky for English speakers. The only way to acquire perfect pronunciation is to spend a considerable amount of time in a Portuguese-speaking country. Nevertheless, if this guide is carefully followed, you should have no problems being understood.

Vowels

Without a doubt the most frustrating thing in learning to pronounce Portuguese is the vowels. The following lists offer only general rules, which should at least enable you to be understood.

a	as the 'u' in 'up'
e	at the beginning or at the end of a word, as the 'ee' in 'feet', only shorter; elsewhere as the 'e' in 'pet'
i	as the 'ee' in 'feet', only shorter
o	at the end of a word or before an **e**, as the 'u' in 'put', only shorter; elsewhere as the 'o' in 'or'
u	as the 'u' in 'put'

Nasalisation

When a tilde appears over a vowel (ã), this means that the vowel should be heavily nasalised. This is done by allowing air to escape through the nose when you are pronouncing the vowel. The sound produced is very similar to the sound you get when you hold your nose and talk. Basically the best way to learn is to listen to Brazilians speaking, and then just practise until you get it right.

7

Diphthongs

Most diphthongs, or combinations of vowels, are pronounced by
following the general rules for vowels, and simply pronouncing
them one after the other in the order that they appear. All the same,
there are a few that are worth noting.

ei	ⱯY	as the 'ay' in 'day', but perhaps a little longer
oi	ᴑY	as the 'oy' in 'boy'
au	ꝒꞪꞮꞮ	as in 'how'
ão		as the 'ow' in 'how', only nasalised
õe	ᴑY	nasalised version of **oi**
ãe	ᴎY	similar to the 'ay' in 'day', only nasalised

Consonants

Most consonants in Portuguese are similar to their English coun-
terparts, but there are exceptions. The good news is that the
consonants are not as difficult to master as the vowels. Only those
consonants which vary considerably from English are discussed
here.

c	as the 'c' in 'cease' when it occurs before **e** or **i**; else-where, as the 'k' in 'kiss'
ç	as the 'c' in 'cease'
d	as the 'j' in 'jungle' when followed by **e** or **i**; elsewhere as the 'd' in 'dog'
g	as the 'g' in 'rouge' when it occurs before **e** or **i**; elsewhere as the 'g' in 'game'
h	not pronounced (see **lh** and **nh**)

j	as the 'g' in 'rouge'
l	after a vowel, something like the 'l' in 'pool', only a bit more like a 'w'; elsewhere, as a regular English 'l'
lh	as the 'lli' in 'million'
m & n	after a vowel, the vowel is nasalised, and the **m** or the **n** is not articulated – a little like the 'ng' in 'sing'; elsewhere, as in English
nh	as the 'ny' in 'canyon'
q	as the 'k' in 'keep'
qu	as 'qu' in 'quill' when followed by **a** or **o**; elsewhere like an English 'k'
r	at the beginning or end of a word as **rr**; elsewhere as a short rolled 'r'
rr	as an English 'h', only with more friction; a little softer than a French 'r' (occasionally you may hear it rolled depending on which part of the country you are in)
s	as the 's' in 'star' before a vowel; before **p**, **t**, **k**, or at the end of a word, as the 'sh' in 'ship'; elsewhere as the 'z' in 'zoo', only a little softer
ss	as the 's' in 'star'
t	as the 'ch' in 'chair' when followed by **e** or **i**; elsewhere as the 't' in 'table'
x	• as the 'sh' in 'ship' when it occurs at the beginning of a word or comes after **e**, **ai**, **ei**, **ou** or **n**
	• as the 'x' in 'taxi'
	• as the 'z' in 'zoo' in the initial syllable **ex**, when followed by a vowel: exam, *exame, (eh-zah-me)*; exercise, *exercício, (eh-zer-see-seeo)*
	• as 'ss' in many words: next, *próximo, (pro-ssee-mo)*; maximum, *máximo, (mah-ssee-mo)*

Stress

When a word ends in **-r** or a nasalised vowel, the stress falls on the last syllable, unless there is an accent on one of the other vowels in the word.

If a vowel has either a circumflex accent (**ê**) or an acute accent (**é**), the stress falls on that vowel no matter where it is in the word. In all other words of more than one syllable, the stress falls on the second-to-last vowel. In the following list the stressed syllable is highlighted:

favour	*fa**vor***
tomorrow	*ama**nhã***
orphan	***ór**fã*
you	*vo**cê***
tear (from the eyes)	***lá**grima*
paragraph	*pa**rá**grafo*
however	*po**rém***

Grammar

Forming Sentences

In general, Portuguese word order is similar to English word order:

My name is Mark.   *Meu nome é Marcos.*
I want to phone the USA.   *(Eu) quero telefonar para os*
   (lit: States United)   *Estados Unidos.*

As in English, word order is subject-verb-object. You will notice that the name for the USA is 'States United'. This is the most obvious difference in word order between Portuguese and English – the adjective comes after the noun:

I am looking for a very   *(Eu) estou procurando um*
   cheap hotel.   *hotel muito barato.*
                    (I am looking for a hotel
                    very cheap)

11

You'll also notice that the word for 'I', *Eu*, is in brackets in the examples given here. This is because it is not usually necessary to include pronouns in sentences where grammatical context makes their identity obvious. As you will find in the section on verbs, the form of the verb tells you who or what the speaker is talking about. If you want to include the pronoun, it is not incorrect.

We are going to Rio de Janeiro tomorrow.	*(Nós) vamos ao Rio de Janeiro amanhã.*
I am hungry.	*(Eu) estou com fome.*

Articles

There are four definite articles in Portuguese. They are:

the (f, sg)	*a*	the woman	*a mulher*
the (f, pl)	*as*	the women	*as mulheres*
the (m, sg)	*o*	the man	*o homem*
the (m, pl)	*os*	the men	*os homens*

There are also four indefinite articles in Portuguese:

a, one (f, sg)	*uma*	a girl	*uma menina*
some (f, pl)	*umas*	some girls	*umas meninas*
a, one (m, sg)	*um*	a boy	*um menino*
some (f, pl)	*uns*	some boys	*uns meninos*

Nouns
Plurals

In general nouns are made plural by adding an *-s*. For example:

| cat | *gato* | cats | *gatos* |
| pen | *caneta* | pens | *canetas* |

If the noun ends in *-s*, *-z* or *-r*, and that syllable is stressed, then the plural is formed by adding *-es*. For example:

woman	*mulher*	women	*mulheres*
Englishman	*inglês*	Englishmen	*ingleses*
youth	*rapaz*	youths	*rapazes*

Gender

There are guidelines by which you can determine the gender of some nouns, but most of them have exceptions.

- Nouns ending with *-dade* are feminine:
  the university   *a universidade*
- Nouns ending with *-ão* are feminine or masculine:
  the hand   *a mão* (f)
  the airplane   *o avião* (m)
- Most nouns ending with *-a* are feminine:
  (the) music   *a música*
- Nouns ending in *-ema*, *-oma* and *-ama* are masculine:
  the cinema   *o cinema*
  the diploma   *o diploma*
  the programme   *o programa*
- Nouns ending with *-o* are masculine:
  the book   *o livro*

Adjectives

Adjectives take the same gender and number as the noun which they describe. They are generally placed after the noun:

a cold beer	*uma cerveja gelada* (a beer cold)
the beautiful beaches	*as praias bonitas* (the beaches beautifuls)
the white wine	*o vinho branco* (the wine white)
an American bank	*um banco americano* (a bank American)

Pronouns
Personal Pronouns

I/me	*eu/mim*	we/us	*nós*
you (sg)	*você*	you (pl)	*vocês*
he/him/it (m)	*ele*	they/them (m)	*eles*
she/her/it (f)	*ela*	they/them (f)	*elas*

Possessive Pronouns

Possessive pronouns work like adjectives, in that they take the gender and number of the noun which they modify. The following table gives both the masculine and feminine singular forms of the possessive pronouns. Plural forms are made by adding *-s*.

	masculine	feminine
my	*meu*	*minha*
your (sg)	*seu*	*sua*
his/her	*seu*	*sua*
our	*nosso*	*nossa*
your (pl)	*seu*	*sua*
their (m/f)	*seu*	*sua*

Remember that possessive pronouns do not vary according to the gender of the possessor, but according to that of the possessed.

Possession can also be expressed by using *de* (of) followed by the relevant personal pronoun or a noun. *De* is contracted to *d* where the personal pronoun begins with a vowel.

The backpack is his.	*A mochila é dele.*
	or *É sua mochila.*
It is their (the girls') car.	*O carro é delas.*
	or *É seu carro.*
It's my passport.	*O passaporte é meu.*
	or *É meu passaporte.*

It can sometimes be an advantage to use *de* plus a personal pronoun or a noun, as this makes the possessor easier to identify. For example, in the sentence 'his/her house is near here', *a sua casa é perto daqui*, the possessive pronoun, *sua*, agrees with the word 'house', *casa*, and we are unable to identify the gender of the owner of the house. If we use, instead, the *de* plus personal pronoun, we get the sentence 'her house is near here', *a casa dela é perto daqui*, and we have the gender of the owner. By using a noun, in this case the woman's name, the owner is identified.

His/Her house is near here.	*A **sua** casa é perto daqui.*
Her house is near here.	*A casa **dela** é perto daqui.*
His house is near here.	*A casa **dele** é perto daqui.*
Madalena's house is near here.	*A casa **de Madalena** é perto daqui.*

Verbs

Verbs, due to their complexity, are probably the aspect of Portuguese that English speakers have the greatest difficulty in mastering. Firstly, there are three standard kinds of regular verbs, depending on whether their infinitives end in *-ar*, *-er* or *-ir*. In addition, there are the double stemmed *-iar* and *-ear* verbs, and the so-called two-stem *-ir* verbs. Finally, there are also irregular verbs.

So, before even contemplating the various tenses and verb forms, there are seven types of verb to cope with. Each of these verb types has 23 possible forms. In all, that comes to a horrifying grand total of 161 possible forms.

Fortunately, only a few of these are essential. Basically all that a visitor needs to know is how to form the future, present and past tenses from the three standard kinds of verbs.

Present

The most important thing in forming the present tense of a verb is to find the stem of the verb by removing its ending (*-ar*, *-er*, *-ir*, etc). For example:

	Infinitive	Stem
to dwell (in a place)	*morar*	*mor-*
to eat	*comer*	*com-*
to leave	*partir*	*part-*

To form the present and the present continuous tenses, various endings are added to the stem, but the endings vary depending on whether the verb ends in *-ar*, *-er* or *-ir*:

Infinitive:	morar	comer	partir
Stem:	mor-	com-	part-
I	-o	-o	-o
he/she/it/you (sg)	-a	-e	-e
we	-amos	-emos	-imos
they/you (pl)	-am	-em	-em

They live in Australia.	*Eles moram na Austrália.*
I do not eat meat.	*Eu não como carne.*
We are leaving now.	*Nós partimos agora.*

Past
This is the most difficult concept to pick up in Portuguese. There are three ways of referring to the past, and in two cases the tense is formed by adding endings to the stem of the verb.

Simple Past If you want to talk about something that is over and done with, then you should add the following endings to the stems:

Infinitive:	morar	comer	partir
Stem:	mor-	com-	part-
I	-ei	-i	-i
he/she/it/you (sg)	-ou	-eu	-iu
we	-amos	-emos	-imos
they/you (pl)	-ram	-ram	-ram

I lived in the USA for one year.	*Eu morei nos Estados Unidos durante um ano.*
They ate alot yesterday.	*Eles comeram muito ontem.*
Helena watched a good film last week.	*Helena assistiu a um bom filme na semana passada.*

This form is also used where English uses 'I have (done, etc)':

Have you read this book?	*Já leu este livro?*

Imperfect This is the other form of the past, constructed by adding the following endings to the verb stems:

Infinitive:	*morar*	*comer*	*partir*
Stem:	*mor-*	*com-*	*part-*
I	*-ava*	*-ia*	*-ia*
he/she/it/you (sg)	*-ava*	*-ia*	*-ia*
we	*-ávamos*	*-íamos*	*-íamos*
they/you (pl)	*-avam*	*-iam*	*-iam*

This is used when you want to describe past actions, or to talk about what used to happen in the past:

I used to drink a lot. (but I don't anymore)	*Antes eu bebia muito.*
She always had lunch at home. (but now she doesn't)	*Ela sempre almoçava em casa.*
You used to open the shop early. (but you don't anymore)	*Você abria a loja cedo.*

You also use the imperfect tense when you want to describe what was happening at a particular point in the past when an action occurred:

I was studying when Maria arrived.	*Eu estudava quando Maria chegou.*

Future
The simplest way to form the future tense is to add the following endings to the infinitive, whether it be an *-ar, -er* or *-ir* verb:

Infinitive:	*morar*	*comer*	*partir*
Stem:	*mor-*	*com-*	*part-*
I		-ei	
he/she/you (sg)		-á	
we		-emos	
they		-ão	

These future tense verb endings are stressed. In the following examples, the stressed syllable has been highlighted:

I will leave tomorrow. *Eu partir**ei** amanhã.*

You will eat beans every day in Brazil. *Você comer**á** feijão todos os dias no Brasil.*

We will sleep well tonight. *Nós dormir**emos** bem hoje à noite.*

They will go to São Paulo in the morning. *Eles/elas ir**ão** para São Paulo de manhã.*

The future tense can also be formed by using the present tense of the verb 'to go', *ir*, followed by the infinitive of the relevant verb. An irregular verb, *ir* is particularly useful and not very difficult:

I am going to leave tomorrow. *Eu vou partir amanhã.*

You are going to eat beans every day in Brazil. *Você vai comer feijão todos os dias no Brasil.*

We are going to sleep well tonight. *Nós vamos dormir bem hoje à noite.*

They are going to go to São Paulo in the morning. *Eles vão para São Paulo de manhã.*

To Be

Portuguese has two verbs which translate as 'to be' in English: *ser* and *estar*. It may take years for an English speaker to master these two completely, but to grasp the basic differences is not too difficult.

Ser

The verb *ser* is an irregular verb, which means that there are no simple rules to follow in declining it. The present tense is declined as follows:

I am	*eu sou*
you are, he/she is	*você é, ele/ela é*
we are	*nós somos*
they are	*eles/elas são*

This verb refers to states which have a degree of permanency or durability about them. For example:

My name is Mark.	*Meu nome é Marcos.*
I am Australian.	*Sou Australiano.*

There is an implication that the states referred to in these two examples will not change.

Estar

The verb *estar*, also meaning 'to be', generally refers to events which are temporary in nature. It is also irregular, but not terribly difficult to learn:

I am	*eu estou*
you are, he/she is	*você/ele/ela está*
we are	*nós estamos*
they are	*eles/elas estão*

Here are some examples of how *estar* is used:

I am lost.	*Estou perdido.*
My friend is ill.	*Meu amigo está doente.*

There is an implication that the states referred to in these two examples may change.

Questions

Questions are often identical to statements, with the exception that the intonation changes. This is done much the same as in English, with a kind of inquisitive rise in the voice at the end of the question.

Are we going to Rio de Janeiro tomorrow?	*(Nós) vamos ao Rio de Janeiro amanhã?*

Question Words

where
  Where is the Australian
    Embassy?

onde
  Onde fica a Embaixada
    Australiana?

when
  When is it necessary to
    renew my visa?

quando
  Quando é preciso renovar
    meu visto?

why
  Why are we stopping here?

por que
  Por que estamos parando
    aqui?

what
  What's wrong?/What's the
    matter?

(o) que
  O que é?/Que é?

how, by what means
  How do I find the bus
    station from here?

como é que
  Como é que vou para a
    rodoviária daqui?

who
  Who are you?

quem
  Quem é você?

which/what (one)
  What's the best restaurant
    in the city?

qual
  Qual é o melhor
    restaurante da cidade?

which/what (ones)
  Which are the best bars in
    the city?

quais
  Quais são os melhores
    bares da cidade?

Greetings & Civilities

Greetings

Hello.	*Olá. Oi.*
Good morning.	*Bom dia.* (relatively formal)
Good afternoon/evening.	*Boa tarde.* (after midday)
Good evening/night.	*Boa noite.* (after dark)
Hi.	*Oi.* (informal, friendly)

All of these greetings (especially the last) are often followed by the question *tudo bem?* or *tudo bom?*, which is something like 'how's things?' or 'how's it going?'. This question doesn't have to be answered, but it would be impolite not to respond to the greeting.

Hi. How's it going?	*Oi. Tudo bem?*
How are you?	*Como está? Como vai?*
I'm well, thanks.	*Vou bem, obrigado/a.*

When someone enquires about your health, as in most countries, there is an expectation that you will respond positively and leave it at that.

good	*bom*
bad	*mau*
terrible	*ruim* (a favourite among Brazilians), or *terrível*

25

Goodbyes

Goodbye.	*Tchau.* (informal)
	Adeus. (formal, more final than *tchau*)
See you soon.	*Até logo.*
See you later.	*Até já.*
Until we meet again.	*Até a próxima.* (informal)

Civilities

Please.	*Por favor.*
No problem/That's alright/ Think nothing of it, etc	*De nada.*
Sorry.	*Desculpe.*
Can you forgive me?	*Você me desculpa?*
Excuse me. (eg when leaving the table)	*Com licença.*

Males and females have different ways of saying 'thankyou'.

Thankyou. (females)	*Obrigada.*
Thankyou. (males)	*Obrigado.*
Many thanks. (females)	*Muito obrigada.*
Many thanks. (males)	*Muito obrigado.*

Forms of Address

Senhor functions as 'Mr', 'Sir' and even 'Lord' (as in 'The Lord's Prayer'). *O senhor* is something like 'gentleman'. It is commonly used when enquiring about someone's health in a particularly respectful manner.

Senhora functions as Mrs, Madam or Ma'am. *A senhora* is something like 'lady'. It is also common when asking respectfully about someone's health:

How are you Sir?	*Como vai o senhor?*
	(lit: How is the gentleman?)
How are you Madam?	*Como vai a senhora?*
	(lit: How is the lady?)

Rapaz is like 'young man'. *Senhorita* is used in Brazil as the equivalent of 'Miss', but it is not particularly widespread. *Menina*

is a young lady or a little girl. *Moça* or *garota* means young woman, young lady. *Rapariga* in Portugal means 'girl', however it should not be used in Brazil as it is extremely disrespectful.

Small Talk

In conversation, Brazilians utilise almost every part of their bodies. Many Westerners (particularly the English speakers) feel uncomfortable when speaking with Brazilians, complaining that they stand too close when talking. Brazilian women often have trouble with Western men, who almost invariably misread their body language. So it is important, during conversation, to be prepared for people standing closer to you than you may be accustomed, and to be aware that it is quite normal behaviour.

Outside the larger cities, where there are not as many travellers, people will be genuinely interested in you and your country.

What is your name?	*Como é seu nome?*
My name is …	*Meu nome é …*

Nationalities

If someone asks you where you are from, the answer depends on the gender and number of your country. For example, Brazil is masculine singular *(o Brasil)*, whereas the USA is masculine plural *(os Estados Unidos)*. Australia is feminine singular *(a Austrália)*, and the Philippines are feminine plural *(as Filipinas)*. As it happens, most countries are feminine singular, but there are too many exceptions for this to be a rule.

So if you are from the USA, you will say *sou dos Estados Unidos*; a Canadian will say *sou do Canadá*; and someone from the UK will say *sou do Reino Unido*.

29

Where are you from?	*De onde você é?*
I am from …	*Sou d-…*
Argentina	*a Argentina*
Australia	*a Austrália*
Brazil	*o Brasil*
Canada	*o Canadá*
Chile	*o Chile*
Denmark	*a Dinamarca*
England	*a Inglaterra*
Finland	*a Finlândia*
France	*a França*
Germany	*a Alemanha*
Ireland	*a Irlanda*
Israel	*Israel*
Italy	*a Itália*
Japan	*o Japão*
New Zealand	*a Nova Zelândia*
Norway	*a Noruega*
Paraguay	*o Paraguai*
Peru	*o Peru*
Scotland	*a Escócia*
Sweden	*a Suécia*
Switzerland	*a Suíça*
the Philippines	*as Filipinas*
the UK	*o Reino Unido*
the USA	*os Estados Unidos*

Occupations

What is your profession?	*Qual é a sua profissão?*
What do you do?	*Que é que você faz?*
Where do you work?	*Onde é que você trabalha?*

The following list includes both male and female forms. Where the name of an occupation ends in a consonant, the feminine form is created by the addition of an 'a'; where it ends in an 'o', turn the 'o' into an 'a'; other vowels remain the same for both forms.

I am a/an ...	*Sou ...*
artist	*artista*
businessperson	*negociante*
doctor	*médico*
journalist	*jornalista*
lawyer	*advogado* (m)
	advogada (f)
mechanic	*mecânico* (m)
	mecânica (f)
nurse	*enfermeiro* (m)
	enfermeira (f)
student	*estudante*
teacher	*professor* (m)
	professora (f)
worker	*trabalhador* (m)
	trabalhadora (f)

Religion

The majority of Brazilians are Catholics. Brazilian Catholicism is heavily influenced by some forms of African and native American animism.

What is your religion?	*Qual é a sua religião?*
I am not religious.	*Não sou religioso/a.*

I am (a/an) ...	*Sou ...*
Anglican	* anglicano/a*
Buddhist	* budista*
Catholic	* católico/a*
Christian	* cristão*
Hindu	* hindu*
Jewish	* judeu*
Muslim	* muçulmano/a*
Protestant	* protestante*

Family

aunt	*tia*
brother	*irmão*
child	*criança*
cousin	*primo/a*
father	*pai*
father-in-law	*sogro*
husband	*esposo*
mother	*mãe*
mother-in-law	*sogra*
nephew	*sobrinho*
niece	*sobrinha*
sister	*irmã*
uncle	*tio*
wife	*esposa*

Language Difficulties

I don't speak Portuguese.	*Não falo portuģuês.*
I don't understand.	*Não compreendo/Não entendo.*
Could you repeat that please?	*Pode repetir, por favor?*
Could you please speak a little more slowly?	*Pode falar mais devagar, por favor?*

Do you speak …?	*Você fala …?*
I speak …	*Eu falo …*
Arabic	*árabe*
Brazilian/Portuguese	*brasileiro/português*
Danish	*dinamarquês*
English	*inglês*
French	*francês*

German	*alemão*
Italian	*italiano*
Japanese	*japonês*
Norwegian	*norueguês*
Spanish	*espanhol*
Swedish	*sueco*

Some Useful Phrases

How old are you?	*Quantos anos você tem?*
I am (25) years old.	*Tenho (vinte e cinco) anos.*
Are you married?	*Vocé é casado/a?*
Do you have any children?	*Você tem filhos?*
Where do you live?	*Onde é que você mora?*

Getting Around

In general, the car driver is king of the road. Other vehicles and pedestrians are often shown no mercy, and certainly no courtesy, and traffic laws are not always respected. Nevertheless, despite all appearances to the contrary, Brazil, in theory at least, does hold to the convention that a red light is a signal to stop.

Watch out at night for cars driving without headlights. It's also always a good idea to slow down as you enter a town; many have *quebra-molas* (speed humps) which you don't see until it's too late.

Directions

east	*leste*
north	*norte*
south	*sul*
west	*oeste*
left	*esquerda*
right	*direita*
straight ahead	*direto, em frente*

Air

There are several major domestic carriers in Brazil, along with smaller domestic airlines. There is also a fleet of air taxis which fly almost anywhere.

When is the next flight to …?	*Quando sai o próximo vôo para …?*
What time does the flight leave?	*A que horas sai o vôo?*
I want to reserve a flight to …	*Quero reservar um vôo para …*
Which airlines fly to …?	*Quais são as companhias aéreas que voam para …?*
How long does the flight take?	*Quanto tempo demora o vôo?*
Will the flight leave on time?	*O vôo sairá na hora?*
Have they delayed the flight?	*Adiaram o vôo?*
How long has the flight been delayed?	*Por quanto tempo foi adiado o vôo?*
I would like a one-way ticket to …	*Quero uma passagem de ida para …*
How much is a return ticket to …?	*Quanto custa uma passagem de ida e volta para …?*
I have a 'Brazil Air Pass'.	*Tenho um 'Brasil Air Pass'.*
Do you need my passport?	*Precisa do meu passaporte?*

Bus

For most Brazilians, buses are the only affordable form of long-distance transport. Bus services are generally excellent. The buses are clean and comfortable and the drivers are usually good.

In every big city, and most small ones, there is a main bus terminal known as a *rodoviária*. The *rodoviárias* are usually on the outskirts of the city.

There are two kinds of long-distance buses. The cheapest and most common is called a *comum*. It is reasonably comfortable and often has air-conditioning and a toilet. The other kind of bus, the *leito* or *executivo*, is truly luxurious. It costs twice as much as a *comum*, but with fully reclining seats, blankets and pillows and, more often than not, a steward serving drinks, it is well worth the splurge for a longer journey.

Where is the bus station?	*Onde é a rodoviária?*
What companies have buses to …?	*Quais são as companhias que têm ônibus para …?*
I want to go to … by leito (comum).	*Quero ir para … de leito (comum).*
How much is the fare?	*Quanto é a passagem?*
What time does the bus leave?	*A que horas sai o ônibus?*
What time does the bus arrive in …?	*A que horas chega o ônibus em …?*
How long does the trip take?	*Quanto tempo demora a viagem?*
How many stops are there on the way?	*Quantas paradas tem no caminho?*

Local Bus

Local bus services tend to be pretty good in Brazil. Since most Brazilians take the bus to work everyday, municipal buses are usually frequent and their network of routes is comprehensive. They are also always cheap and crowded.

Does this bus go to …?	*Este ônibus vai para …?*
What bus goes to …?	*Qual é o ônibus que vai para …?*
How much is the fare?	*Quanto é a passagem?*
Can you tell me when we get to …?	*Pode me dizer quando chegamos a …?*
Excuse me, I want to get off the bus here.	*Com licença, quero descer do ônibus aqui.*

Taxi

The taxis in big cities tend to have meters which are updated by a *tabela* that converts the price on the meter to a new price – the inflation rate is so high that the meters cannot be updated fast enough. If the taxi doesn't have a meter, or it doesn't work, negotiate a fare before getting in.

Where can I find a taxi?	*Onde é que posso encontrar um táxi?*
Can you take me to …?	*Pode me levar para …?*
How much would it cost to go to …?	*Quanto custa para ir a …?*
That is too much.	*É demais.*
I need a taxi to go to the airport.	*Preciso de um táxi para ir ao aeroporto.*

How much do I owe you?	*Quanto lhe devo?*
Can you wait here for 10 minutes?	*Pode esperar aqui por dez minutos?*

Instructions

Stop at the next corner please.	*Pare na próxima esquina, por favor.*
Turn left/right here.	*Dobre à esquerda/direita aqui.*
Continue straight ahead.	*Sempre em frente.*
Take the second side street on the right.	*Tome a segunda travessa à direita.*

Car

Renting a car is expensive; prices are comparable with those in the USA and Europe. Volkswagen bugs (called *fuscas* in Brazil) are the cheapest cars to rent.

Where can I rent a car?	*Onde é que posso alugar um carro?*
I would like to rent a car.	*Queria alugar um carro.*
How much is the rental for one day (one week)?	*Quanto é o aluguel por um dia (uma semana)?*
Does that include mileage?	*Isso inclui a kilometragem?*
What kind of car do you have for hire?	*Que tipo de carro tem para alugar?*
Where can I buy some petrol?	*Onde é que posso comprar gasolina?*
How much does petrol cost?	*Quanto custa a gasolina?*
Do I need insurance?	*Preciso de seguro?*

Some Useful Words

accident	*acidente*
bicycle	*bicicleta*
bus (local)	*ônibus*
bus (long-distance)	*ônibus comum, leito, executivo*
car	*carro, automóvel*
corner	*esquina*
highway	*estrada, auto-estrada*
motorcycle	*motocicleta*
one-way street	*rua de mão única*
pedestrian	*pedestre*
pedestrian/zebra crossing	*cruzamento*
street	*rua*
taxi	*táxi*
traffic	*trânsito*
traffic light	*sinal (de trânsito)*
tram/streetcar	*bonde*
truck	*caminhão*

Accommodation

The cost and standard of accommodation in Brazil can be incredibly varied. There are five-star hotels in Rio, São Paulo and Brasília which are as expensive and luxurious as any in the world; while there are huts, *barracas,* in some of the smaller Amazonian towns which are nothing more than four posts holding up a thatched roof under which to sling your hammock.

Luxuries such as hot running water and flushing toilets cannot be guaranteed in any of the cheaper hotels, *hotéis,* and boarding houses, *pensões,* although most places south of Bahia tend to be more aware of the needs of tourists. In the interior, the north-east, and the north of Brazil, even the wealthier locals don't often have hot running water in their homes. But then, with the sometimes stifling humidity, a cold shower two or three times a day can be a real godsend.

The word *hotel* is also the generic term for any form of travellers' accommodation. Youth hostels are not very common in Brazil; they are generally found only in the larger cities of the south.

Finding Accommodation

I am looking for ...	*Estou procurando ...*
a hotel	*um hotel*
the Youth Hostel	*o Albergue de Juventude*
a boarding house	*uma pensão*
somewhere to spend the night	*onde passar a noite*

I'm looking for a cheap hotel. — *Estou procurando um hotel barato.*

It must not be too expensive. — *Não deve ser muito caro.*

At the Hotel

I would like a room please. — *Quero um quarto, por favor.*

Could I see the room? — *Posso ver o quarto?*

How much does it cost per night/week? — *Quanto é a diária/semana?*

Don't you have anything cheaper? — *Não tem nada mais barato?*

Is there a discount? — *Tem desconto?*

Can you give me a better price? — *Pode fazer um melhor preço?*

Is that with breakfast? — *É com a café da manhã?*

Do you have full board? — *Tem pensão completa?*

Does it have air-conditioning? — *Tem ar condicionado?*

Requests & Complaints

Does the room have a bathroom?	*O quarto tem banheiro?*
Is there hot water?	*Tem água quente?*
Is the hot water turned on all day?	*A água quente está ligada o dia inteiro?*
I'd like a room with a good view.	*Quero um quarto com uma boa vista.*
I've lost the key to my room.	*Perdi a chave do meu quarto.*
Do you have a safe where I can leave my valuables?	*Tem um cofre onde posso guardar minhas coisas de valor?*
Could you make up my bill please?	*Pode preparar minha conta, por favor?*
Do you accept credit cards?	*Você aceita cartão de crédito?*
The room is too noisy.	*O quarto é barulhento demais.*
The light doesn't work.	*A luz não funciona.*
The room is dirty.	*O quarto está sujo.*
The fan is broken.	*O ventilador está quebrado.*
broken	*quebrado*
dark	*escuro*
dirt	*sujeira*
dirty	*sujo*
noise	*barulho*
noisy	*barulhento*
smell	*cheiro*

Some Useful Words

air-conditioning	*ar condicionado*
balcony	*terraço*
bath	*banho*
bathroom	*banheiro*
bed	*cama*
candle	*vela*
chair	*cadeira*
double bed	*cama de casal*
fan	*ventilador*
mirror	*espelho*
shower	*ducha/chuveiro*
soap	*sabonete*
table	*mesa*
toilet	*banheiro*
toilet paper	*papel higiênico*
towel	*toalha*
wardrobe	*guarda-roupa*
window	*janela*

Most showers in Brazil use electricity to heat the water. The element is contained within the shower rose, and when the tap is turned on, the water pressure in the shower head trips a switch and the water is heated. Don't touch the shower rose when the water is running, as it is possible to receive an electric shock. Always turn the water off prior to adjusting the temperature.

Around Town

If you ask Brazilians to give you directions, it is almost certain that they will comply. The only problem is that people will often go out of their way to give an answer, even if they don't know where your destination is. It pays to ask more than one person. Of course, if you end up with three sets of directions to the one place, you are no better off than when you started. A rule of thumb, followed by many long-term foreign residents, is to keep asking until you get the same answer three times.

Could you tell me where … is?	*Pode me dizer onde fica …?*
Where is …?	*Onde fica …?*
the bank	*o banco*
the bus stop	*o ponto de ônibus*
the (Argentinian) consulate	*o consulado (argentino)*
the (Venezuelan) embassy	*a embaixada (venezuelana)*
the market	*o mercado*
I am looking for …	*Estou procurando …*
a hospital	*um hospital*
my hotel	*o meu hotel*
the post office	*o correio*
the police station	*a delegacia (de polícia)*
a public telephone	*um telefone público*
the tourist office	*a agência de turismo*

At the Bank

Changing money in Brazil is easy in the large cities. Almost anyone can direct you to a money exchange house, *casa de câmbio*. You can also change money at most banks, and travellers' cheques at some (ask before you sign your cheque). When you do exchange money, ask for lots of small bills, as change, *troco* or *miúdo*, is often unobtainable at newsagents, restaurants, in taxis, etc (or so they will tell you).

In small towns without a bank, you'll have to ask around – there is usually someone who buys cash dollars. Changing money at weekends, even in the big cities, can be extremely difficult, so make sure you have enough to last until Monday.

I want to change some money.	*Quero trocar dinheiro.*
I want to change a/some travellers' cheque(s).	*Quero trocar um/alguns cheque(s) de viagem.*

Some Useful Words

bank	*banco*
black market	*mercado paralelo*
cashier/teller	*caixa*
commission	*comissão*
credit card	*cartão de crédito*
exchange rate	*taxa de câmbio*
money (general)	*dinheiro*
coin	*moeda*
note	*nota*

Black Market

Changing money on the black market in Brazil is illegal. This doesn't stop anyone making black market transactions, but it is worth choosing your contact carefully. The exchange rate on the black market varies, at a higher rate than the official rate, depending on political tensions and the demand for hard currency, among other things.

To get an idea of what the US dollar is worth on the black market, just buy a copy of one of the major regional newspapers. The black market rate is generally printed alongside the official rate in the finance section of the paper. Of course this will only give you a rough idea. Travellers' cheques generally pay less than cash.

Don't, under any circumstances, change money on the streets, follow exchangers into unfamiliar areas, or give money or unsigned cheques upfront.

Do you know where I can change some dollars?	*Sabe onde posso trocar alguns dólares?*
Will you change travellers' cheques?	*Você troca cheques de viagem?*
How much will you give me for each dollar?	*Quanto é que você me dá por cada dólar?*
Do you have change?	*Tem troco?*

At the Post Office

Postal services are pretty good in Brazil. Most mail seems to get through, and airmail letters to the USA and Europe usually arrive in a week or so. For Australia, allow two weeks. The cost, however, is ridiculously high for mail leaving Brazil.

There are mail boxes on the street but it's a better idea to go to a post office. Most post offices, *correios*, are open Monday to Friday from 9 am to 6 pm, and Saturday morning.

I would like some stamps.	*Quero alguns selos.*
I would like to send a letter to (Australia).	*Quero mandar uma carta para (a Austrália).*
I would like to send it registered mail please.	*Quero mandar registrado, por favor.*
How much does it cost to send this to (England)?	*Quanto custa mandar isto para (a Inglaterrra)?*

Some Useful Words

airmail	*via aérea*
letter	*carta*
package	*um pacote*
postcard	*um cartão postal*
poste restante	*posta restante*
surface mail	*via superfície*
telegram	*telegrama*

Telephone

Local calls in Brazil are very cheap. They can be made from public phones in the street or at telephone centres. Special coins, *fichas telefônicas*, are needed for this purpose, and can be bought from most newsstands or in telephone centres.

Long-distance calls within Brazil are reasonably priced considering the size of the country. Although it is possible to call long distance from some street phones, the *fichas* run out very quickly. International call tariffs are exorbitant.

Many telephone centres are open 24 hours. The queues can be very long during the day, so it might be a good idea to wait until late evening to make your call. This varies, however, from region to region.

I would like to speak to (Senhor Gonçalves).	*Queria falar com o (Senhor Gonçalves).*
Hello, is (Sandra) there?	*Alô, a (Sandra) está?*
I would like to make a reverse-charges (collect) call to (Canada).	*Queria telefonar a cobrar para (o Canadá).*
How much does it cost per minute?	*Quanto custa por minuto?*
What time is it in (California) now?	*Que horas são na (Califórnia) agora?*

Some Useful Words

engaged (occupied)	*ocupado*
public telephone	*orelhão/telefone público*
telephone book	*catálogo telefônico*
telephone call	*telefonema*
telephone coin	*ficha telefônica*

Security

Personal security is a major concern for the traveller in Brazil. Unfortunately, with poverty as widespread as it is, theft is a common occurrence. Good advice for travellers is to leave any jewellery or expensive watches at home.

Violent crime is a very real problem in Brazil. Think twice before wandering into a slum, *favela*, alone. Also make sure that you always (and that means always) have some money on you. If someone does stick a gun in your face, the last thing you want to say is that you left all your money at the hotel.

If you must walk around alone at night in the big cities, try to stick to the well-lit areas. Women need to be doubly careful.

Leave me alone (in peace).	*Me deixa em paz.*
Don't bother me.	*Não amola.*
Help!	*Socorro!*
I've been robbed.	*Me roubaram.*
They took ...	*Levaram ...*
my money	*meu dinheiro*
my passport	*meu passaporte*

assault	*assalto*
insurance	*seguro*

knife	*faca*
pistol	*pistola*
thief	*ladrão*

Some Useful Phrases

What time does it open?	*A que horas abre?*
What time does it close?	*A que horas fecha?*
Where must I go to extend my visa?	*Para onde é que preciso ir para renovar meu visto?*
I would like to extend my visa.	*Queria renovar meu visto.*

In the Country

Weather

Boy it's hot today! (a common complaint from taxi drivers)	*Como está quente hoje! Que calor danado!* (somewhat stronger)
The wind is very strong.	*O vento está bem forte.*
It's raining.	*Está chovendo.*
Are you hot/cold?	*Está com calor/frio?*
I'm hot/cold.	*Estou com calor/frio.*
The sun is very strong.	*O sol está bem forte.*

Some Useful Words

cloud	*nuvem*
rain	*chuva*
rainbow	*arco-íris*
snow	*neve*
storm	*tempestade*
sun	*sol*
weather	*tempo*
wind	*vento*

Animals, Birds & Insects

animal	*animal*
bird	*ave, passarinho*
butterfly	*borboleta*
cat	*gato*
chicken	*galinha, frango*
cow	*vaca*
dog	*cachorro, cão*
fish	*peixe*

fly	*mosca*
lizard	*lagarto*
mosquito	*mosquito*
ox	*boi*
pig	*porco*
sheep	*carneiro*
snake	*cobra, serpente*
spider	*aranha*

Plants

cactus	*cacto*
carnation	*cravo*
coconut palm	*coqueiro*
daisy	*margarida*
flower	*flor*
guava tree	*goiabeira*
jackfruit tree	*jaqueira*
mango tree	*mangueira*
palm tree	*palmeira*
pine	*pinho*
rose	*rosa*
sugar cane	*cana de açúcar*
tree	*árvore*

Some Useful Words

beach	*a praia*
city	*a cidade*
farm	*a fazenda*
hill	*o morro*
hinterland/bush	*o sertão, o interior*

jungle	*a selva*
mountain	*a montanha*
ocean	*o oceano*
plain	*a planície*
river	*o rio*
swamp/marsh/wetlands	*o pantanal*
village	*a vila/o povoado/ a cidadezinha*
wave (of sea)	*a onda*

Food

The staple foods in Brazil are beans, *feijão*, rice, *arroz*, noodles, *macarrão* and manioc flour, *farinha de mandioca*. For some, the addition of meat to these staples is an uncommon luxury. The cheapest meat is chicken, *frango*, but pork, *carne de porco*, is also a fairly common staple for those with a little extra to spend. There is plenty of beef, *carne de boi*, in Brazil.

At the Restaurant

One thing you will notice about Brazil is the variety of eating establishments. Seafood restaurants can also be reasonably priced.

Could I see the menu please?	*Posso ver o cardápio/o menu, por favor?*
I would like the soup of the day please.	*Queria a sopa do dia, por favor.*
I am a vegetarian.	*Sou vegetariano/a.*
I can't eat meat.	*Não posso comer carne.*
Not too spicy please.	*Não muito picante, por favor.*
Could you please bring some salt and pepper?	*Pode trazer sal e pimenta, por favor?*
Could you bring the bill please?	*Pode trazer a conta, por favor?*

Bread	**Pão**
sweet bread	*pão doce*
toast	*torrada*
Dairy Products	**Laticínios**
butter	*manteiga*
cheese	*queijo*
goat's cheese	*queijo de cabra*
milk	*leite*
yoghurt	*iogurte*
Eggs	**Ovos**
egg	*ôvo*
boiled egg	*ôvo cozido*
fried egg	*ôvo frito*
poached eggs	*ovos quentes*
scrambled eggs	*ovos mexidos*
Meat	**Carne**
beef	*carne de boi*
chicken	*frango, galinha*
mutton	*carne de carneiro*
pork	*carne de porco*
Seafood	**Peixe & Marisco**
fish	*peixe*
fried fish	*peixe frito*
grilled fish	*peixe grelhado*
cod	*bacalhau*
crab	*caranguejo*

lobster	*lagosta*
oyster	*ostra*
shellfish	*marisco*
trout	*truta*

Vegetables

Legumes

bean	*feijão*
carrot	*cenoura*
cauliflower	*couve-flor*
corn	*milho*
cucumber	*pepino*

garlic	*alho*
green vegetables	*verduras*
lettuce	*alface*
mushroom	*cogumelo*
onion	*cebola*
pumpkin	*abóbora*
vegetable	*legume*

Regional Dishes – National

churrasco – basically barbecued meat, especially beef. The best places to try it are called *churrascarias.*

feijoada – could almost be considered the national dish. It is a bean-based meal with bits of meat (mainly pork, sausage, and sometimes beef) and various other ingredients. It is always served with rice and *farofa*, which is manioc flour fried with onion and egg. Beyond that there is no hard and fast recipe; rather it contains whatever the family can afford. It can be fairly stodgy, and very spicy. No trip to Brazil is complete without trying this at least once and it's very likely that you will eat it on numerous occasions.

siri – stuffed crab. You can often find this in beachfront restaurants.

Regional Dishes – North-East & Bahia

acarajé – another bean-based dish with salt, onions, palm oil and peppers. It also often contains shrimps.

agulha – a very thin fish that looks a little like a garfish. It is barbecued and, if you're lucky, brought to you on the beach. You eat the entire thing, head, bones and all. It is definitely more of a snack than a full meal.

carne de sol or *carne sêca* – a very salty meat; definitely not for anyone with hardening arteries. It is generally grilled and served with an assortment of beans, rice and vegies. The closest thing I know of in the West is beef jerky.

moqueca – a seafood stew which can contain a variety of seafoods such as lobster, octopus, squid, oyster, crab, or whatever fish came in on the fishing boat that morning. It is heavily flavoured with tomato, onion, coriander, some kind of citrus fruit juice, salt, and Brazil's favourite – coconut milk.

sarapatel – a definite favourite in Bahia, though it is certainly not to every visitor's liking. It is basically a mixture of pork giblets, pork lard, blood, mint leaf and an assortment of spices.

sururu – a very tasty mussel dish

tapioca – found mainly in the north and, especially, north-east. It is the Brazilian equivalent of a taco. Basically it is a manioc-flour pancake which is cooked over an open fire in a frying pan. The most likely place to find it is in markets, or somewhere outside where the locals hang out in the evening. As a delicious option you might ask for it with cheese, *com queijo*, in which case it is fried with an enormous lump of fresh goat's cheese in the middle.

vatapá – consists of shrimp, herring and cashew nuts, with a garlic, pepper, coconut milk and palm oil sauce. Delicious!

xinxim de galinha – chicken and shrimp in a sauce of onion, garlic, coriander, palm oil, salt and pepper.

Condiments	Molhos
chilli sauce	*molho picante*
honey	*mel*
mustard	*mostarda*

pepper	*pimenta*
salt	*sal*
sugar	*açúcar*
vinegar	*vinagre*

Fruit   Fruta

The incredible diversity of fruits in Brazil never ceases to amaze
the visitor. Almost the entire country is in the tropics, so tropical
fruits are certainly the most abundant. However, in the region
south of São Paulo, there are huge orchards full of the temperate
fruits that you find all over the USA, Australia and Europe. Some
fruit found only in the northern regions will send your tastebuds
into a frenzy.

apple	*maçã*
apricot	*damasco*
avocado	*abacate*
banana	*banana*
breadfruit	*fruta pão*
coconut	*côco*
grape	*uva*
guava	*goiaba*
honeydew melon	*melão*
lemon	*limão*
mango	*manga*
orange	*laranja*
papaya	*mamão*
peach	*pêssego*
pear	*pera*

pineapple	*abacaxi*
plum, prune	*ameixa*
strawberry	*morango*
tangerine	*tangerina*
tomato	*tomate*
watermelon	*melancia*

Tropical Fruits

biribá – an Amazonian fruit, which is eaten plain

cacau – produces the seeds from which chocolate is made. The pulp from the cocoa pod tastes wonderfully sweet and creamy, not a bit like cocoa.

caju – looks like a red or yellow pepper with a kidney on top. The 'kidney' is roasted, then split open to reveal a single cashew nut. The fruit makes a wonderful juice when mixed with a little sugar. Some people like to eat the fruit plain, although it has a tart taste like a cross between a lemon and a pear.

fruta de conde or *pinha* – a very popular sweet fruit from the apple family

graviola – a large fruit with bumpy green skin and yellow flesh, known as custard apple. It makes a delicious ice cream.

jaca – jackfruit. The flesh is rubbery and sweet, and rather strongly flavoured. It also makes a great ice cream.

Sweets & Desserts   *Doces*

Many sweets can be bought over the counter in bakeries, *padarias*. The variety can be a bit daunting, but most people seem to get what they want simply by pointing.

cake	*bolo*
ice cream	*sorvete*
sweet	*doce*

Brazilian ice creams are a delight. In the best ice-cream parlours, *sorveterias*, you might find up to 50 different flavours. Most of them are made from tropical fruit and are often distinctly Brazilian.

Drinks   *Bebidas*
Nonalcoholic
Drinking coffee is another not-to-be-missed experience in Brazil. Most people drink it very strong and very sweet, so if you want

it some other way you'll have to make it very clear. If you say nothing you will certainly get sugar.

coffee (small, strong, sweet)	*cafezinho*
black coffee (with sugar)	*café puro*
instant coffee	*nescafé*
white coffee	*café com leite*
milk	*leite*
mineral water	*água mineral*
with gas	*com gás*
without gas	*sem gás*
tea	*chá*
water	*água*
without sugar	*sem açúcar*

In Brazil you will find all the soft drinks that you know so well back home – Coca-Cola, 7-UP, Fanta (there is also grape Fanta), etc. Undoubtedly the king of soft drinks in Brazil, however, is *guaraná*. There are a few companies that make this drink, but the best are Brahma and Antártica. Look out for these.

You can also buy powdered guaraná, *guaraná em pó*, which you mix up like a cordial, adding sugar to taste. Made from an Amazonian berry, it is said to be very high in vitamins, and can be found all over the country.

Alcoholic

Brazilian beers are pretty good. The national favourites are Cerpa, Antártica and Brahma Chopp (pronounced 'shopee').

Brazilian wines from the south are quite good. You can also get imported wines if you want to splurge – Portuguese or Chilean wines offer the best value for money.

beer	*cerveja*
white wine	*vinho branco*
red wine	*vinho tinto*

When Brazilians want to get rolling drunk without spending too much, they drink *cachaça* (also known as *pinga* or *aguardente*). It is a very high-proof, sugar-cane alcohol. You need an asbestos stomach to drink any large quantities of this stuff straight. Still, it makes for a really potent mixer and is certainly much more palatable that way.

A popular and delicious drink is *caipirinha*, a mixture of crushed lime, sugar, *cachaça* and ice. It goes well with *feijoada*, and anytime as a refreshing alcoholic drink.

Shopping

Bargaining

Bargaining is pretty much the standard way of doing any small business transaction in Brazil. The most common place for this kind of transaction is either in a market or in a small shop. In department stores or food shops, prices are set.

How much does this cost?	*Quanto custa isso?*
That is very expensive.	*É muito caro.*
That is too expensive for me.	*Isso é caro demais para mim.*
I found it cheaper in another shop.	*Achei mais barato numa outra loja.*
Can you bring the price down a little?	*Pode baixar o preço um pouco?*
I will give you 5000 cruzeiros.	*Dou cinco mil cruzeiros.*
It costs 10,000 cruzeiros.	*Custa dez mil cruzeiros.*

Clothing

Clothing in Brazil can vary quite considerably in quality. Like anywhere else, if you buy the cheapest clothes on the market in Brazil they invariably fall apart before too long. Brazil is the world's largest wholesale manufacturer of shoes, however, unless you have changed your money on the black market, you will not find them particularly cheap.

bathing suit	*roupa de banho*
bikini	*bikini, tanga*
coat	*casaco*
dress	*vestido*
hat	*chapéu*
jacket	*paletó*
pullover	*pullover*
sandals	*sandálias*
shirt	*camisa*
shoes	*sapatos*
shorts	*calção, short*
skirt	*saia*
socks	*meias*
tights	*meia-calça*
trousers	*calças*
underwear	*roupa íntima*

Brazilian beaches (particularly Copacabana and Ipanema) are famous for a daring bikini known as *fio dental*, literally 'dental floss'.

Stationery & Publications

exercise book	*caderno*
guidebook	*guia*
magazine	*revista*
map	*mapa*
newspaper	*jornal*
notebook	*agenda*
novel	*romance*
pen	*caneta*

| pencil | *lápis* |
| writing paper | *papel de carta* |

Colours

black	*preto/a*
blue	*azul*
brown	*marrom (castanho* for eyes or hair)
green	*verde*
grey	*cinza*
orange	*cor laranja*
pink	*rosa*
purple	*roxo/a*
red	*vermelho/a*
white	*branco/a*
yellow	*amarelo/a*

Weights & Measures

The metric system is fairly universal in Brazil, although cheese is often measured in pounds, *libras*.

centimetre	*centímetro*
metre	*metro*
kilometre	*kilômetro*
gram	*grama*
kilogram	*kilo*

Sizes & Comparisons

| big | *grande* |
| bigger | *maior* |

biggest	*o/a maior*
small	*pequeno/a*
smaller	*menor*
smallest	*o/a menor*
heavy	*pesado/a*
heavier	*mais pesado/a*
light	*leve*
lighter	*mais leve*
long	*comprido/a*
tall	*alto/a*
short	*curto/a* (in stature: *baixo/a*)
few	*poucos/poucas*
some	*alguns/algumas*
much	*muito*
many	*muitos/muitas*
thin	*magro/a*
thick	*grosso/a*
fat	*gordo/a*
fast	*rápido*
slow	*devagar*

Some Useful Phrases

I would like to buy …	*Queria comprar …*
Do you have this in another colour?	*Tem isso de outra cor?*
Don't you have a cheaper one?	*Não tem mais barato?*
I'm just looking.	*Estou só olhando.*
It is too big/too small for me.	*É grande demais/pequeno demais para mim.*

Could you wrap it please?	*Pode embrulhar, por favor?*
Do you have a bag?	*Tem uma sacola?*
I want that one please.	*Quero aquilo, por favor.*
Could you show me another one?	*Pode me mostrar outro?*
Where can I find …?	*Onde posso encontrar …?*
Do you have books in English?	*Tem livros em inglês?*

Some Useful Words

brush	*escova*
button	*botão*
comb	*pente*
department store	*loja de departamento*
market	*mercado*
needle	*agulha*
shop	*loja*
soap	*sabonete*
thread	*linha*
toilet paper	*papel higiênico*
toothbrush	*escova de dentes*
toothpaste	*pasta dental*

Health

Some private medical facilities in Rio de Janeiro and São Paulo are on par with any good Western hospital, but you should be wary of public hospitals in the interior. They are notorious for re-using syringes after quick dips in alcohol baths, for lack of soap, and other unsanitary practices. University hospitals are likely to have English-speaking physicians, while UK and US consulates have lists of English-speaking physicians.

I need a doctor.	*Preciso de um médico.*
Where can I find a good doctor?	*Onde posso encontrar um bom médico?*
Could you please call a doctor?	*Você pode chamar um médico, por favor?*
I need a dentist.	*Preciso de um dentista.*
Is there a hospital near here?	*Tem um hospital aqui perto?*

At the Doctor

I am ill.	*Estou doente.*
My friend (female) is ill.	*Minha amiga está doente.*
My friend (male) is ill.	*Meu amigo está doente.*
I have a vaccination certificate.	*Tenho um certificado de vacinação.*
I have my own syringe.	*Tenho minha própria seringa.*
I have a prescription (for it).	*Tenho receita médica (para isso).*

71

At the Chemist
Many drugs which require a prescription in the developed world can be bought over the counter in any pharmacy in Brazil. Generic names for various pharmaceuticals can vary from one country to another, so be aware of what it is that you are buying. Also check the use-by date as Brazil's climate causes things to go off rather quickly.

I need something for a cold.	*Preciso de alguma coisa para o resfriado.*
Do I need a prescription for ...?	*Preciso de uma receita para ...?*

Ailments

allergy	*alergia*
anaemia	*anemia*
asthma	*asma*
burn	*queimadura*
constipation	*prisão de ventre*
cough	*tosse*
cramp	*cãibra*
diarrhoea	*diarréia*
dysentery	*disenteria*
fever	*febre*
headache	*dor de cabeça*
infection	*infecção*
itch	*coceira*
malaria	*malária*
pain	*dor*
rash	*erupção/irritação na pele*

stomachache	*dor de barriga*
sunburn	*queimadura de sol*
sunstroke	*insolação*
toothache	*dor de dente*
yellow fever	*febre amarela*

Parts of the Body

arm	*braço*
back	*costas*
blood	*sangue*
bone	*osso*
chest	*peito*
ear	*ouvido* (inner ear), *orelha*
eye	*olho*
foot	*pé*
hand	*mão*
head	*cabeça*
heart	*coração*

knee	*joelho*
leg	*perna*
mouth	*boca*
nose	*nariz*
shoulder	*ombro*
stomach	*estômago*
teeth	*dentes*
throat	*garganta*

Some Useful Words

accident	*acidente*
antibiotics	*antibióticos*
antiseptic	*anti-séptico*
aspirin	*aspirinas*
bandage	*atadura*
blood test	*análise de sangue*
broken	*quebrado/a*
condoms	*preservativo*
contraceptive	*anticoncepcional*
faeces	*fezes*
injection	*injeção*
injury	*ferimento*
medicine	*remédio*
nurse	*enfermeira*
tablet	*comprimido*
tampon	*tampão*
urine	*urina*
wound	*ferida*

Time & Dates

Telling the Time

The word *horas*, meaning 'hours', is instrumental in telling the time.

What time is it?   *Que horas são?*

There are two possible ways to answer this question. If it is any hour other than 1 o'clock, whether am or pm, the answer uses a plural form of the verb 'to be', *ser*. Otherwise the singular form is used. Rather than dividing the day into am and pm, in Portuguese you say 'of the morning', *da manhã*, from midnight until midday; 'of the afternoon', *da tarde*, from midday until sunset, and 'of the night', *da noite*, from sunset until midnight.

It is ...   *É ...*
  1 pm   *uma hora da tarde*
  1 am   *uma hora da manhã*
  midnight   *meia-noite*
  midday   *meio-dia*

It is ...   *São ...*
  7 am   *sete (horas) da manhã*
  2 pm   *duas (horas) da tarde*
  11 pm   *onze (horas) da noite*

6.25 am	*seis (horas) e vinte e cinco da manhã*
3.30 pm	*três (horas) e meia da tarde*
8.15 pm	*oito (horas) e quinze da noite*
9.40 pm	*nove (horas) e quarenta da noite*

Sometimes the 24-hour clock is used, in which case it is not necessary to use *da manhã, da tarde* or *da noite*. See the Numbers chapter for all the remaining numbers that can be used for telling the time.

Days of the Week
Monday	*segunda-feira*
Tuesday	*terça-feira*
Wednesday	*quarta-feira*
Thursday	*quinta-feira*
Friday	*sexta-feira*
Saturday	*sábado*
Sunday	*domingo*

Months
January	*janeiro*
February	*fevereiro*
March	*março*
April	*abril*
May	*maio*
June	*junho*
July	*julho*
August	*agosto*

September	*setembro*
October	*outubro*
November	*novembro*
December	*dezembro*

Dates

What date is it?	*Que data é hoje?*
It is ...	*Hoje é ...*
30 March	*trinta de março*
Monday 21 July	*segunda feira, vinte e um de julho*

Present

now	*agora*
today	*hoje*
tonight	*hoje de noite*
this morning	*hoje de manhã*
this week	*esta semana*
this ycar	*este ano*
this month	*este mês*

Past

yesterday	*ontem*
the day before yesterday	*há dois dias (atrás)*
a few days ago	*faz alguns dias*
yesterday morning	*ontem de manhã*
yesterday evening	*ontem à noite*
last week	*a semana passada*
last month	*o mês passado*
last year	*o ano passado*

just before	*faz pouco tempo*
quite a while ago	*faz bastante tempo*
long ago	*faz muito tempo*

Future

tomorrow	*amanhã*
day after tomorrow	*depois de amanhã*
tomorrow afternoon	*amanhã de tarde*
tomorrow morning	*amanhã de manhã*
next week	*a semana que vem*
next month	*o mês que vem*
next year	*o ano que vem*
later	*depois, mais tarde*

Some Useful Words

day	*dia*
morning	*manhã*
afternoon	*tarde*
evening/night	*noite*
week	*semana*
month	*mês*
year	*ano*
not yet	*ainda não*
everyday	*todos os dias*
always	*sempre*
never	*nunca*

Numbers & Amounts

Cardinal Numbers

0	*zero*
1	*um* (m), *uma* (f)
2	*dois* (m), *duas* (f)
3	*três*
4	*quatro*
5	*cinco*
6	*seis*
7	*sete*
8	*oito*
9	*nove*
10	*dez*

11	*onze*
12	*doze*
13	*treze*
14	*catorze/quatorze*
15	*quinze*
16	*dezesseis*
17	*dezessete*
18	*dezoito*
19	*dezenove*
20	*vinte*
21	*vinte e um*
22	*vinte e dois*
23	*vinte e três*
30	*trinta*
31	*trinta e um*
40	*quarenta*
50	*cinqüenta*
60	*sessenta*
70	*setenta*
80	*oitenta*
90	*noventa*
100	*cem*
101	*cento e um*
115	*cento e quinze*
146	*cento e quarenta e seis*
200	*duzentos*
300	*trezentos*
400	*quatrocentos*
500	*quinhentos*
600	*seiscentos*

700	*setecentos*
800	*oitocentos*
900	*novecentos*
1000	*mil*
2000	*dois mil*
3568	*três mil quinhentos e sessenta e oito*
100,000	*cem mil*
500,000	*quinhentos mil*
one million	*um milhão*

Ordinal Numbers

Ordinal numbers are masculine (ending in -*o*) or feminine (ending in -*a*), according to the gender of the noun they qualify.

1st	*primeiro/a*
2nd	*segundo/a*
3rd	*terceiro/a*
4th	*quarto/a*
5th	*quinto/a*
6th	*sexto/a*
7th	*sétimo/a*
8th	*oitavo/a*
9th	*nono/a*
10th	*décimo/a*
11th	*décimo primeiro/a*
12th	*décimo segundo/a*
20th	*vigésimo/a*
24th	*vigésimo quarto/a*
30th	*trigésimo/a*

Fractions

¼	*um quarto*
⅓	*um terço*
½	*meio*
1½	*um e meio*

Some Useful Words

count	*contar*
number	*número*
very	*muito*
few	*poucos/poucas*
many	*muitos/muitas*
some	*alguns/algumas*
how many?	*quantos?/quantas?*
how much?	*quanto? quanto é?*
too much	*demais*
enough	*bastante*

Vocabulary

A

able – *capaz*
accept – *aceitar*
accident – *acidente*
actor – *ator/atriz*
address – *endereço*
aeroplane – *avião*
afraid – *com medo*
after – *depois*
airport – *aeroporto*
aspirin – *aspirina*
aunt – *tia*

B

baby – *bebê, neném*
bad – *mau*
bag – *bolsa, sacola*
bank – *banco*
because – *porque*
before – *antes*
bicycle – *bicicleta*
birthday – *aniversário*
blood – *sangue*
book – *livro*
boy – *rapaz, moço*
boyfriend – *namorado*

bring – *trazer*
broke (without money) – *liso, duro*
brush – *escova*
burn (n) – *queimadura*
burn (v) – *queimar*
busy (telephone) – *ocupado*
buy – *comprar*

C

camera – *máquina fotográfica*
candle – *vela*
car – *carro*
centre – *centro*
cheap – *barato/a*
chemist – *farmácia*
child – *criança*
choose – *escolher*
Christmas – *Natal*
church – *igreja*
cinema – *cinema*
city – *cidade*
clean – *limpo/a*
clothing – *roupa*
c/o (care of) – *aos cuidados de*
collect (reverse-charges) – *a cobrar*

congratulations – *parabéns*
cook – *cozinhar*
country – *país* (eg Australia), *campo* (ie rural area)
couple (noun) – *casal*
cry – *chorar*
cycle – *andar de bicicleta*

D

daily – *diário*
damage – *dano*
dance – *dançar*
dark – *escuro*
darling – *querido/a*
date – *data*
daughter – *filha*
dawn – *madrugada*
day – *dia*
dead – *morto/a*
debt – *dívida*
decide – *decidir*
deep – *fundo*
delay – *adiar*
demand – *exigir*
dentist – *dentista*
depart – *partir*
describe – *descrever*
develop (a film) – *revelar*
diamond – *diamante*
dinner – *jantar*

dirty – *sujo*
disagree – *não concordar, discordar*
disease – *doença*
dizzy – *tonto/a*
doctor – *médico/a*
dog – *cão, cachorro*
doll – *boneca*
door – *porta*
dormitory – *dormitório*
down(ward) – *para baixo*
dream – *sonho*
dress – *vestido*
drive – *dirigir*
drum – *tambor*
drunk – *bêbado/a*
dry – *seco/a*

E

each – *cada*
early – *cedo*
earn – *ganhar*
easy – *fácil*
Easter – *Páscoa*
eat – *comer*
edge – *borda*
election – *eleição*
electricity – *eletricidade*
electric shock (to receive) – *tomar um choque (elétrico)*

elevator (lift) – *elevador*
embassy – *embaixada*
emerald – *esmeralda*
employee – *empregado/a*
employer – *patrão/patroa*
empty – *vazio*
end – *fim*
engaged (telephone) – *ocupado*
enjoy – *divertir, curtir*
enough – *bastante, suficiente*
envelope – *envelope*
every – *cada*
everybody – *todos*
everything – *tudo*
except – *exceto, menos*
exit – *saída*
eye – *olho*

F

face – *rosto*
faint – *desmaiar*
faithful – *fiel*
family – *família*
fan – *ventilador*
far – *longe*
fare – *passagem*
farm – *fazenda*
fast – *rápido*
father – *pai*

fence – *cerca*
festival – *festa, festival*
fever – *febre*
fiancé – *noivo*
fiancée – *noiva*
fight – *luta*
film (photographic) – *filme*
fine (penalty) – *multa*
finger – *dedo*
fire – *fogo*
flavour – *sabor*
flower – *flor*
flu – *gripe*
food – *comida*
foreigner – *estrangeiro/a*
forget – *esquecer*
fork – *garfo*
fresh – *fresco/a*
friend – *amigo/a*
fruit – *fruta*
full – *cheio/a*
funny – *engraçado/a*
furniture – *móveis*

G

game – *jogo*
garbage – *lixo*
garden – *jardim*
garlic – *alho*
gate – *portão*

gemstone – *pedra (semi) preciosa*
girl – *moça, garota*
girlfriend – *namorada*
give – *dar*
glove – *luva*
glue – *cola*
go – *ir*
goal – *gol*
goalkeeper – *goleiro*
God – *Deus*
gold – *ouro*
good – *bom/boa*
government – *governo*
grandchild – *neto/a*
grandparents – *avós*
grill – *grelhar*
guard – *guarda*
guitar – *violão*

H

hair – *cabelo*
hairdresser – *cabeleireiro/a*
happen – *acontecer*
happy – *feliz*
hate – *odiar*
have – *ter*
head – *cabeça*
health (also 'cheers' when drinking) – *saúde*
hear – *ouvir*
heavy – *pesado/a*
help! – *socorro!*
here – *aqui*
hiccups – *soluços*
hill – *morro, colina*
hitchhike – *pedir carona*
holiday – *férias*
honest – *honesto/a*
hope – *esperar*

house – *casa*
humid – *úmido*
hungry – *com fome*
hunt – *caçar*
husband – *marido*

I

ice – *gelo*
ice cream – *sorvete*
ill – *doente*
illegal – *ilegal*
immediately – *imediatamente*
inch – *polegada*
increase – *aumentar*
injection – *injeção*
injury – *ferida*
ink – *tinta*
insect – *inseto*
insurance – *seguros*
iodine – *iodo*
iron (clothes) – *passar (roupa)*

J

jail – *prisão*
jealous – *ciumento/a*
jewel – *jóia*
job – *trabalho*
joke – *brincadeira, piada*
juice – *suco*

K

keep – *guardar*
key – *chave*
kick (football) – *chutar*
kill – *matar*
kitchen – *cozinha*
knife – *faca*
knock (on the door) – *bater (na porta)*
know (someone, a place) – *conhecer*
know (something) – *saber*

L

lake – *lago*
lamp – *lâmpada*
landslide – *desmoronamento (de terra)*
language – *língua*
last – *último*
late – *tarde*
laugh – *rir*
laundry – *lavanderia*
law – *lei*
lazy – *preguiçoso/a*
leaf – *folha*
letter – *carta*
lid – *tampa*
life – *vida*
lift (elevator) – *elevador*

like (v) – *gostar de*
live (to inhabit) – *morar*
lock – *fechar à chave*
look – *olhar*
lose – *perder*
lost – *perdido*
love – *amar*
lunch – *almoço*

M

machine – *máquina*
magazine – *revista*
mail – *correio*
make – *fazer*
make-up – *maquiagem*
man – *homem*
manager – *gerente, diretor*
married – *casado/a*
marry – *casar*
match (for lighting) – *fósforo*
mattress – *colchão*
meat – *carne*
medicine – *remédio*
mend – *consertar*
menu – *menu, cardápio*
milk – *leite*
mirror – *espelho*
mistake – *erro*
money – *dinheiro*
more – *mais*
mother – *mãe*

mouse – *rato, camundongo*
moustache – *bigode*
move – *mudar*
much – *muito/a*

N

near – *perto de*
nearly – *quase*
necklace – *colar*
nephew – *sobrinho*
never – *nunca, jamais*
new – *novo/a*
news – *notícias*
next – *o próximo*
nice – *simpático, bonito, bom*
niece – *sobrinha*
no – *não*
noodles – *macarrão*
nose – *nariz*
nothing – *nada*
now – *agora*

O

octopus – *polvo*
offend – *ofender*
offer – *oferecer*
office – *escritório*
official – *oficial*
often – *muitas vezes, com frequência*

oil – *óleo*
old – *velho/a*
olive – *azeitona*
only – *só/somente*
open – *aberto*
operation – *operação*
opportunity – *oportunidade*
or – *ou*
orphan – *órfão/órfã*
outside – *fora*
oven – *forno*
owe – *dever*

P

packet – *pacote*
page – *página*
pain – *dor*
paint – *tinta*
painting – *quadro, pintura*
pale – *pálido/a*
pants – *calças*
paper – *papel*
parade – *desfile*
parcel – *pacote, embrulho*
parents – *pais*
party – *festa*
passenger – *passageiro/a*
path – *caminho*
patient – *paciente*
pay – *pagar*
pedestrian – *pedestre*

pen – *caneta*
people – *gente*
pepper – *pimenta*
perhaps – *talvez*
person – *pessoa*
petrol – *gasolina*
place – *lugar*
plan – *plano*
plate – *prato*
pocket – *bolso*
poor – *pobre*
pregnant – *grávida*
prisoner – *prisioneiro*
probably – *provavelmente*
profit – *lucro*
pub – *bar*
purse – *bolsa, bolsinha*
pyjamas – *pijama*

Q

question – *pergunta*
quickly – *rapidamente*
quiet – *tranqüilo/a*

R

rabbit – *coelho*
railway – *estrada de ferro*
rain – *chuva*
rape – *violentar, estuprar*
raw – *cru*

read – *ler*
ready – *pronto*
reason – *razão*
receipt – *recibo*
reef – *recife*
remember – *lembrar*
restaurant – *restaurante*
rich – *rico/a*
ring – *anel*
ripe – *maduro/a*
risk – *risco*
river – *rio*
roast – *assar*
rob – *roubar*
robber – *ladrão*
robbery – *roubo*
rubbish – *lixo*
rude – *mal educado/a*
run – *correr*

S

sad – *triste*
salad – *salada*
same – *mesmo/a*
sand – *areia*
sauce – *molho*
say – *dizer*
scenery – *paisagem*
school – *escola*
scratch (verb) – *arranhar*
  (noun) – *arranhão*

sea – *mar*
season – *estação*
seat – *assento, lugar*
see – *ver*
send – *mandar, enviar*
servant – *empregado/a*
sew – *coser, costurar*
shade – *sombra*
sheep – *carneiro*
shellfish – *marisco*
ship – *navio, barco*
shop – *loja*
shut – *fechar*
side – *lado*
silver – *prata*
simple – *fácil, simples*
sit – *sentar*
size – *tamanho*
sleep – *dormir*
slowly – *devagar*
small – *pequeno/a*
smoke – *fumar*
soap – *sabonete*
soap opera – *novela*
song – *canção*
soon – *logo*
sound – *som*
souvenir – *lembrança*
speak – *falar*
spoon – *colher*
sport – *esporte*
star – *estrela*

stay – *ficar*
steal – *roubar*
street – *rua*
strong – *forte*
sugar – *açúcar*
suntanned – *bronzeado/a*
sweet – *doce*

T

table – *mesa*
tablet – *comprimido*

take – *tomar*
taste – *gosto*
tea – *chá*
thankyou – *obrigado/a*
then (at that time) – *então*
thief – *ladrão*
think – *pensar*
threaten – *ameaçar*
ticket – *bilhete, passagem*
toilet – *banheiro*
tomorrow – *amanhã*
tonight – *hoje à noite*

touch – *tocar*
traffic – *trânsito*
train – *trem*
translate – *traduzir*
travel – *viajar*
truck – *caminhão*
typewriter – *máquina de escrever*

very – *muito*
via – *por, via*
view – *vista*
visa – *visto*
visit – *visitar*
vomit – *vomitar*
voyage – *viagem*

U

ugly – *feio/a*
umbrella – *guarda-chuva*
uncle – *tio*
under – *embaixo de*
understand – *entender, compreender*
unless – *a não ser que, a menos que*
unpack – *desfazer (as malas)*
unripe – *verde*
untidy – *desarrumado*
until – *até*
up – *para cima*
useful – *útil*

W

wage – *salário*
wait – *esperar*
walk – *andar*
wallet – *carteira*
want – *querer*
war – *guerra*
wardrobe – *guarda-roupa*
wash – *lavar*
watch (time) – *relógio*
water – *água*
waterfall – *catarata, cachoeira*
week – *semana*
wet – *molhado/a*
wife – *mulher*
window – *janela*
wood – *madeira*
wool – *lã*
work – *trabalhar*
wrap – *embalar, embrulhar*
write – *escrever*

V

vacancy – *vaga*
vegetable – *legumes*
vegetarian – *vegetariano*

X

x-rays – *raios-x (x* pronounced as 'sheesh')

Y

yacht – *iate*
yam – *inhame*

year – *ano*
yes – *sim*
yesterday – *ontem*
young – *jovem*

Z

zoo – *jardim zoológico*

LONELY PLANET PHRASEBOOKS

Complete your travel experience with a Lonely Planet phrasebook. Developed for the independent traveller, the phrasebooks enable you to communicate confidently in any practical situation – and get to know the local people and their culture.

Skipping lengthy details on where to get your drycleaning ironed, information in the phrasebooks covers bargaining, customs and protocol, how to address people and introduce yourself, explanations of local ways of telling the time, dealing with bureaucracy and bargaining, plus plenty of ways to share your interests and learn from locals.

Arabic (Egyptian)
Arabic (Moroccan)
Australian
  Introduction to Australian English, Aboriginal and Torres Strait languages.
Baltic States
  Covers Estonian, Latvian and Lithuanian.
Bengali
Brazilian
Burmese
Cantonese
Central Europe
  Covers Czech, French, German, Hungarian, Italian and Slovak.
Eastern Europe
  Covers Bulgarian, Czech, Hungarian, Polish, Romanian and Slovak.
Ethiopian (Amharic)
Fijian
Greek
Hindi/Urdu
Indonesian
Japanese
Korean
Lao
Latin American (Spanish)
Mandarin

Mediterranean Europe
  Covers Albanian, Greek, Italian, Macedonian, Maltese, Serbian & Croatian and Slovene.
Mongolian
Nepali
Papua New Guinea (Pidgin)
Pilipino
Quechua
Russian
Scandinavian Europe
  Covers Danish, Finnish, Icelandic, Norwegian and Swedish.
Sri Lanka
Swahili
Thai
Thai Hill Tribes
Tibetan
Turkish
Ukranian
USA
  Introduction to US English, Vernacular Talk, Native American languages and Hawaiian.
Vietnamese
Western Europe
  Useful words and phrases in Basque, Catalan, Dutch, French, German, Irish, Portuguese and Spanish (Castilian).

LONELY PLANET AUDIO PACKS

Audio packs are an innovative combination of a cassette/CD and phrasebook presented in an attractive cloth wallet made from indigenous textiles by local communities.

The cassette/CD presents each language in an interactive format. A number of successful language teaching techniques are used, enabling listeners to remember useful words and phrases with little effort and in an enjoyable way.

Travellers will learn essential words and phrases – and their correct pronunciation – by participating in a realistic story. The scripts have been developed in the belief that the best way to learn a new language is to hear it, then to practise it in the context in which you will use it. The emphasis is on effective communication.

The cassette/CD complements the relevant phrasebook, and the cloth wallet makes the pack an attractive and convenient package – easy to display in shops and useful and practical for travellers.

Cassettes & CDs
- complement phrasebooks
- realistic storylines explore situations that will be useful for all travellers
- languages are spoken by native speakers
- listeners learn key words and phrases in repetition exercises, then hear them used in context
- realistic sound effects and indigenous music used throughout
- length: 80 minutes

Cloth Pack
- ticket-wallet size – suitable for airline tickets, notes etc
- made from traditional textiles woven and sewn by local communities
- cardboard reinforced and sealed in plastic for easy display
- size: 140 x 260 mm

Available now: Indonesian audio pack; Japanese audio pack; Thai audio pack

PLANET TALK

Lonely Planet's FREE quarterly newsletter

Every issue is packed with up-to-date travel news
and advice including:

- a letter from Lonely Planet co-founders Tony and
  Maureen Wheeler
- go behind the scenes on the road with a Lonely
  Planet author
- feature article on an important and topical travel
  issue
- a selection of recent letters from travellers
- details on forthcoming Lonely planet promotions
- complete list of Lonely Planet products

To join our mailing list contact any Lonely Planet office.

LONELY PLANET PUBLICATIONS

AUSTRALIA
PO Box 617, Hawthorn 3122, Victoria
tel: (03) 9819 1877 fax: (03) 9819 6459
e-mail: talk2us@lonelyplanet.com.au

USA
Embarcadero West,
155 Filbert St, Suite 251,
Oakland, CA 94607
tel: (510) 893 8555
TOLL FREE: 800 275-8555
fax: (510) 893 8563
e-mail: info@lonelyplanet.com

UK
10 Barley Mow Passage, Chiswick,
London W4 4PH
tel: (0181) 742 3161 fax: (0181) 742 2772
e-mail: 100413.3551@compuserve.com

FRANCE:
71 bis rue du Cardinal Lemoine, 75005
Paris
tel: 1 44 32 06 20 fax: 1 46 34 72 55
e-mail: 100560.415@compuserve.com

World Wide Web: http://www.lonelyplanet.com